100

THINGS TO DO IN

LOUISVILLE

BEFORE YOU

DIE

2nd Edition

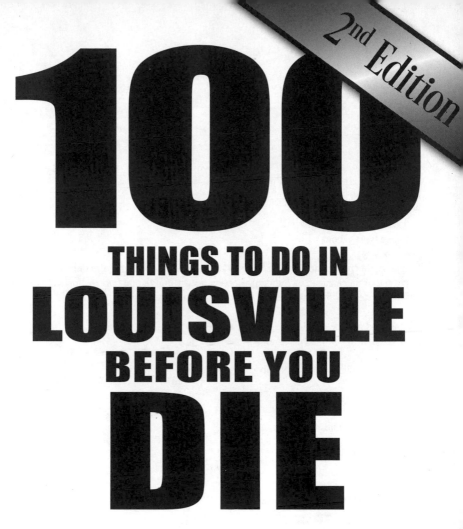

100

THINGS TO DO IN
LOUISVILLE
BEFORE YOU
DIE

2nd Edition

KEVIN GIBSON

REEDY PRESS

Library of Congress Control Number: 2018939879

ISBN: 9781681061566

Design by Jill Halpin

Cover Image: Kevin Gibson

Printed in the United States of America
18 19 20 21 22   5 4 3 2 1

Please note that websites, phone numbers, addresses, and company names are subject to change or cancellation. We did our best to relay the most accurate information available, but due to circumstances beyond our control, please do not hold us liable for misinformation. When exploring new destinations, please do your homework before you go.

DEDICATION

This book is dedicated to Louisville,
the city I proudly call home, and all those who
proudly live here with me.
Oh, and to my dog, Darby. Always.

• •

CONTENTS

Music and Entertainment

Sports and Recreation

• •

Culture and History

• •

Shopping and Fashion

PREFACE

When I first considered presenting *100 Things to Do in Lousville Before You Die,* my worry was how I would ever come up with that many. One hundred? Really? But once I started giving it some serious thought, doing a little research, and talking with other Louisvillians, I began to wonder how on earth could I contain the book to *only* 100. Sadly, many great things about Louisville had to be left out once the smoke had cleared and the book was finished.

Anyway, welcome to Louisville (that's *looey*-ville, in case you're new here). In this book, you'll read about the city's dining scene, nightlife, festivals, ins and outs, ups and downs, interesting characters, historical head-scratchers, and much more. You'll find out about Louisville's impressive arts scene. You'll learn just how fanatical the city is about a single horse race every spring. You'll learn how fanatical it is about bourbon all year long. You'll know that college basketball is king, and it's either red or blue—not both.

I'm quite proud to be the one to write this book, in part because I've lived in the Louisville area all my life. As a result, I feel I've watched it grow into the great city that I truly believe it to be. It's a place where the cost of living is reasonable, you can raise a family comfortably, and never, ever run out of things to do. Truly, there's just so much to do here. I often remark, when talking to friends, "There's something going on every day in Louisville." Seems that's absolutely true: be it a concert or a 5K run, a new restaurant grand

• •

opening or a sporting event, a festival or Churchill Downs After Dark. My city rarely sleeps, as it is one of few in America where the bars stay open until 4 a.m. every night.

As a food and beverage writer, I have the opportunity to take part in plenty of these activities (although, these days, I'm never out until 4 a.m.). I not only go out and do things, but I also see things happening and hear about things happening. New restaurants, new breweries, new bars, new distilleries, and new experiences abound in Louisville. As a journalist of 25+ years in the area, I've covered everything from the arts scene to college basketball. Louisville's diversity has made me professionally diverse. Yet, with all the activity, one can, at any time, find the banks of the Ohio River, sit contemplatively, and wait for the sounds of the riverboats to sweep everything away. Louisville is a beautiful place to simply relax and watch the sun set. Heck, I just hope I can do this city justice.

As you get ready to jump in, whether you're a Louisvillian yourself, a visitor, or someone considering moving to the River City, please know that these 100 things are far from everything Louisville has to offer. These are just some handpicked snapshots—some are obvious, some not so obvious. I had to leave out many good ones, so maybe in a few years I can make another list and write another book. By then, there's no telling how far Louisville will have come.

— Kevin Gibson

• •

ACKNOWLEDGMENTS

I have a huge list of people to thank, in part because I put out a call to my friends for suggestions to make sure I didn't forget anything. I have a lot of friends, and they did not let me down. I'll get to them in a moment, but first, I want to thank my good friend (who is also a great writer) Fred Minnick, who connected me with Reedy Press. I also can't possibly send enough thank-yous to Stacey Yates from the Louisville Convention and Tourism Bureau. In just one lunch, my list doubled, thanks to her. I owe her a beer, and one day I will make good on that debt. In addition, my thanks to Jacob L. Zimmer (LouisvilleKY.photos), who took the cover photograh.

I also want to thank my supportive friends and family, who never give me grief when I say, "I can't today; I have to stay home and write." I especially have to thank Cynthia Bard, who hears those words perhaps more than anyone. I also want to thank Cindy and Jerry Mason for their patience and generosity and, of course, the fine folks at Reedy Press.

As for all those who offered suggestions, I had originally planned to include only the names of the people whose suggestions I actually used, but it dawned on me that I had already earmarked many of the ones I received and didn't want to purposely exclude them simply because I had already thought of it. Also, pretty much all the ideas were really good but just didn't make the cut due to space limitations. So, I decided to include everyone. Here they are, in no particular order, and I apologize unreservedly if I inadvertently left anyone out:

Thanks to Cynthia Bard, Greg Thomas, Jessica Thacker, Jeanette Smith, Kevin J. Gibbs, John Ronayne, Glen Owen, Tracey Coke, Butch Bays, Brenda Skaggs, Chuck Skibo, Maggie Kimbrel, Christy Bradshaw, Bonnie Rae Hoffman, Katricia Melzer, Kory Wilcoxson, Chuck Johnson, Morgan Bard, McKenna Byerly, Gary Dreschel, Heather Leoncini, Stephanie Owen, Glenda Reeves, Robin Garr, Denise Szostak, Eric Belmonte, Chris Noble, Mike Walton, Rick Stidham, Kristen Reinhart Davis, Tisha Michelle Gainey, Kelly Lenfert Hammons, Justin Lewis, Christy Bradshaw, Cindy Smith Bain, Kevin Sparks, Amy Mohs, Ang DeFebbo, Russ Meredith, Jonathan Hodge, Jeremy Sebolt, Rob Marlin, Kim Williams, Tracey Saelen, LeeAnn Tracy Bagby, Kimberly Fisher Mays, Denny Cress, Cathy Cress, Charlie Robbins, Amy Barkley, Alex Gustafson, Shayne Myhand, Melanie Rae, Bob Hill, Tim Burnash, Audria Denker, Bruce Corwin, Nick Landers, Christy Lovell Miley, Dave Hargrave, Rhonda Burks, Kimberly Jo Lawless, Valerie Bott Kincaid, Chuck Kaplan, Don Haag, Tim Estridge, and John King. You guys rock.

• •

FOOD AND DRINK

Photos by Chris Witzke, courtesy of the Brown Hotel

ENJOY A HOT BROWN
AT THE BROWN HOTEL

If you don't know what a Hot Brown is, boy does Louisville have a treat for you. It's a dish native to the Brown Hotel and now a local historic staple, a hearty fest of flavor created by Chef Fred Schmidt in the 1920s to feed late-night revelers at the hotel bar. An open-faced turkey sandwich with bacon and a delicate Mornay sauce, the Hot Brown was an instant hit. When you go, be sure to sit in the lobby bar and get a mint julep in a real sterling silver cup. Enjoy your Hot Brown and consider the history. Then check out the second-floor balcony of the beautiful hotel, from which people actually would fish during the 1937 flood.

335 West Broadway, (888) 888-5252
BrownHotel.co
Downtown

TIP
Check the walls for vintage menus on display that will show you just how much cheaper the original Hot Brown was than the one you just ate.

EAT AN ELEPHANT EAR
AT THE CHOW WAGON

Every year during the Kentucky Derby Festival downtown workers find their way to Waterfront Park during their lunch breaks and during happy hour to have an elephant ear at the Chow Wagon. Or some Italian shaved ice. Or a bratwurst the size of a baby's arm. At night, for the more adventurous Louisvillians and out-of-town guests, the Chow Wagon lights up with live music. It is a staple of the Derby Festival, that magical time of year when there is a massive parade, the Great Steamboat race, the annual Balloon Glow, and more, proving once and for all that the Kentucky Derby is really just an excuse to have a two-week party in preparation for a two-minute race.

Waterfront Park
discover.kdf.org
Downtown
Family Friendly

TIP

Take the kids to the Pegasus Parade on Broadway so they can see the giant inflatables and the colorful floats. The kid inside you might even make an appearance. The Pegasus Parade is always the Thursday before Derby.

DO THE BAMBI WALK, THEN EAT A BURRITO
AS BIG AS YOUR HEAD

That headline says it all. The Highlands area is well known for its late-night fun-seekers, and when they've had enough and need something to warm their bellies, La Bamba, a non-descript Mexican joint near the Mid-City Mall, is where many of them go. The sign touts "Burritos as Big as Your Head!" Weird, but, again, it's 3 a.m., and you've just ingested eight beers and three shots of something green. At this point, you'd eat a dishrag if it had *pico de gallo* on it. It's the perfect end to the famous Bambi Walk, the dive-bar tour that has been a Louisville tradition for decades or even the more recently developed No Cover Walk.

1237 Bardstown Road, (502) 451-1418
LaBambaBurritos.com
Highland

TIP

If your belly can't handle Mexican food at that hour, check out Twig & Leaf just down the street or Burger Boy downtown for some greasy and affordable diner fare. To cure your hangover the next day (and to try to remember why on earth you did that to yourself), hit Barbara Lee's Kitchen in Clifton for breakfast.

DISCOVER
THE LOUISVILLE BREWING SCENE

Craft beer's popularity is ever-growing, and Louisville has plenty of breweries worth checking out. One of the best known is Against the Grain, located inside Slugger Field downtown. With its elevated, Victorian-style brewhouse and spacious environs, it's almost as fun to look at as it is to drink within. But there are plenty of other breweries, including two locations for the city's oldest operating brewpub, Bluegrass Brewing Company. If you stop at Falls City Brewing Company (whose brand dates back to 1905), or at Apocalypse Brew Works, you might get a taste of Kentucky Common, invented in Louisville and one of only two beer styles that originated in North America. You can even catch a bus for a guided tour.

RECOMMENDED BREWERIES

Against the Grain Brewery & Smokehouse
ATGBrewery.com

Bluegrass Brewing Company
BBCBrew.com

Great Flood Brewing
GreatFloodBrewing.com

Falls City Beer
FallsCityBeer.com

Apocalypse Brew Works
ApocalypseBrewWorks.com

Goodwood Brewing Co.
Goodwood.beer

Monnik Beer Co.
Facebook.com/
MonnikBeer

Akasha Brewing Co.
AkashaBrewing.com

New Albanian Brewing Company
NewAlbanian.com

Donum Dei Brewery
Facebook.com/
DonumDeiBrewery

Floyd County Brewing Company
FloydCountyBrewing.com

Flat 12 Bierwerks
Flat12.me

Gordon Biersch
GordonBiersch.com

Holsopple Brewing
HolsoppleBrewing.com

Gravely Brewing Co.
GravelyBrewing.com

Mile Wide Beer Co.
MileWideBeer.com

DIG INTO
A BENEDICTINE SANDWICH

In 1911, a restaurateur named Jennie Carter Benedict opened a tea room on downtown Louisville's South Fourth Street. She created Benedictine, a simple but refreshing green spread made with cream cheese and cucumbers that many consider a cousin to pimento cheese, another Southern spread. Improbably, Benedictine became a Kentucky staple and a treat that most outside the state have never experienced, save for seeing it mentioned in dozens of cookbooks, national news outlets, or on the Food Network. But in Louisville, Benedictine is like, well, ketchup. You can enjoy a fully fresh and local version at Lilly's Bistro in the Highlands or get a downhome version at Frank's Meat & Produce on Preston Highway.

Lilly's Bistro
1147 Bardstown Road, (502) 451-0447
LillysBistro.com

Frank's Meat & Produce
3342 Preston Highway, (502) 363-3989
Highlands/South End
Family Friendly

SATISFY YOUR SWEET TOOTH
WITH A MODJESKA AT MUTH'S

Opened in 1921, Muth's Candies is a long-standing downtown tradition where families go to step back in time, satisfy a sweet tooth, stock up for holiday visitors, or get a few dozen bourbon balls for the annual Derby party. The signature candy at Muth's is a soft deluxe marshmallow treat coated with butter and cream caramel (and some also with chocolate!). The candy was created by Anton Busath at Muth's because, well, he had a celebrity crush. The candy was named after a famous Polish actress named Helena Modjeska, who appeared in Louisville several times in the 1880s. Crush on.

630 E Market Street, (502) 585-2952
MuthsCandy.com
NuLu
Family Friendly

DINE LIKE SINATRA
AT VINCENZO'S

Italian brothers Vincenzo and Agostino Gabriele opened this downtown legend that has played host to the likes of Steven Spielberg, Sylvester Stallone, Tommy Lasorda, and others; it is a classic, upscale Italian restaurant in a gorgeous space. From the ornate bar to the elegant dining room, Vincenzo's is one of those places you go to impress a client or to pop the question. Legend has it that Frank Sinatra himself visited the restaurant in the late 1980s, at which point a special veal dish was created just for him. He liked it so much that he ordered extra to go so he and his band could enjoy it on the road. Because of this, the *Involtini di Vitello Sinatra,* a veal Scallopine dish, came to be a permanent fixture on the menu. Fly your taste buds to the moon.

150 South Fifth Street, (502) 580-1350
VincenzosItalianRestaurant.com
Downtown

SAMPLE ICE CREAM
AT COMFY COW

Comfy Cow is a Louisville original that is fast growing into a regional home of some of the best ice cream you'll ever slurp. Its flagship location is located in the Clifton neighborhood in the buildout of an old home. Impossible to miss thanks to its garish pink color, it is a destination (especially in summer months) for families, couples, joggers, cyclists, and others seeking a soothing taste of, well, pretty much anything. Flavors rotate with favorites, such as Cow Tracks, Mint Chocolate Chippy, Strawberry Fields Forever, and Cookie Monster Dough.

2221 Frankfort Avenue, (502) 409-4616
TheComfyCow.com
Clifton/Crescent Hill
Family Friendly

TIP
Don't be afraid to ask for a sample. Or two. Or three.
The folks at Comfy Cow want you to be happy.

HAVE A BEER, BRUNCH
AT HOLY GRALE AND GRALEHAUS

Leave it to Louisville to be home to a "bed and beverage." Let me explain: the Holy Grale is a craft and imported beer haven in a space that began as a church, built circa early 1900s. The Gralehaus is a coffee shop and brunch eatery that also has guest rooms for rent upstairs, set in an original Victorian home built in 1905. The two share a beer garden, where good times (and good food and good drinks) are had by all. Any questions?

Holy Grale
1034 Bardstown Road, (502) 459-9939
HolyGraleLouisville.com

Gralehaus
1001 Baxter Avenue, (502) 454-7075
Gralehaus.com
Highlands

TIP
Try a pint of your favorite beer with a shot of espresso. Mind blowing.

HAVE GREEN CHILI WONTONS
AT THE ORIGINAL BRISTOL

The original Bristol Bar & Grille, established in 1977, is a Highlands staple, a date-night standard that gets people started on their evening on the town. The signature snacks at the Bristol, with its dark wood finish and white tablecloths, are the Green Chili Wontons. When in Louisville, if you go to the Bristol, you get the wontons; it's just what you do. They're just spicy enough, crispy-meets-gooey little nuggets of Monterey Jack cheese and green chiles that you dip into a house-made guacamole sauce. They're nothing fancy—just a tasty appetizer to get things moving and a Louisville classic that has been copied but never quite matched.

1321 Bardstown Road, (502) 456-1702
BristolBarandGrille.com
Highlands
Family Friendly

HANG OUT
AT THE BAR AT PAT'S STEAKHOUSE

Pat's Steakhouse is a Louisville tradition that goes back more than five decades, set in a coach inn and travelers rest stop that dates back 150 years. The vibe at Pat's is one of quiet serenity, especially on the bar side, where green-jacketed waiters come and go, Sinatra croons over the sound system, and regulars sip bourbon and chat with the bartenders. Old Hollywood photos line the walls, and the bar, incredibly, dates back to 1860. In short, it's the kind of sleek, throwback place where at any given moment you expect to hear someone call a lady a "dame." Sit at the bar, have some baby froglegs or an oyster cocktail, and enjoy the historic trip back in time. (The steaks are really good, too.)

2437 Brownsboro Road, (502) 893-2062
PatsSteakhouseLouisville.com
Clifton/Crescent Hill
Family Friendly

FILL UP
ON LOUISVILLE-STYLE PIZZA

Everyone knows Chicago-style pizza, the hearty, deep-dish pie piled with toppings. There's Detroit-style pizza, St. Louis-style pizza with Provel cheese, stuffed pizza, thin New York-style—you get the idea. Louisville sort of has its own style as well, and there are several places you can score it around town. It all starts with Impellizerri's Pizza, which started back in the 1980s, carrying over to Wick's Pizza and Clifton's Pizza. It's generally thought to be a thick, heavily-topped pie with the cheese placed over the toppings—both in double portions—as opposed to vice-versa as on most pizzas. It's sort of a Louisville comfort food and a staple. Don't leave Louisville without it.

Impellizzerri's Pizza
1381 Bardstown Road (and four other locations)
Impellizzerris.com

Wick's Pizza
975 Baxter Avenue and three other locations
Wickspizza.com

Clifton's Pizza Company
2230 Frankfort Avenue
Cliftonspizza.com
Family Friendly

COMPLETE
THE URBAN BOURBON TRAIL

A cousin to the much-ballyhooed Kentucky Bourbon Trail, which connects distilleries across the state, the urban version requires you to carry a passport or passport app around to any six of the three dozen or so bars and restaurants on the trail to try a bourbon, have a bite to eat, and get your passport stamped. Not only do you get a cross-section of Louisville's bourbon scene, but you also get a free T-shirt for your efforts.

(888) 568-4784
BourbonCountry.com

TIP
Be sure to include the Silver Dollar (WhiskeyByTheDrink.com) on your list, which is revered nationally as one of America's best bourbon bars. It's set in an old firehouse and comes complete with Bakersfield-era country music played on vinyl. Just down the street is Bourbon's Bistro (BourbonsBistro.com), another widely revered Louisville bourbon stop.

HAVE LUNCH AT THE COUNTER
AT MORRIS' DELI AND LIQUORS

Hidden away in the Highlands, Morris' Deli and Liquors is exactly what the name suggests: a place to get a great sandwich that also has a gigantic beer cave. Stop into the unassuming little storefront, grab yourself a beer from the cave (it's *coooold* in there), and then order up the signature country ham sandwich or a pimento cheese sandwich (or maybe both). If you want funky mustards and relishes, just ask, but be careful with those hot pickles. This one's a real Louisville treasure.

2228 Taylorsville Road, (502) 458-1668
Highlands
Family Friendly

PLAY BEERHALLA
AT FRANKFORT AVENUE BEER DEPOT

You've heard of Valhalla, the country club and Jack Nicklaus–designed golf course where a number of PGA events have been held. This is Beerhalla, a well-traveled miniature golf course behind the legendary bar and barbecue joint locals call "the Original F.A.B.D." Bring the kids, play a couple of rounds—watch out for that sixth hole because it's a beast—and then have yourself a brisket sandwich with some spicy green beans on the patio by the palm trees. It's some of the best smoked meat around in a town filled with terrific barbecue.

3204 Frankfort Avenue, (502) 895-3223
FABDSmokehouse.com
Crescent Hill/Clifton
Family Friendly

BUILD YOUR OWN BURGER
AT WW COUSINS

Since 1983, WW Cousins has been the place to go for a good burger, where patrons also can top their own at a huge condiment bar complete with forty free toppings, from the basic iceberg lettuce to spicy mustard and even sauerkraut. WW Cousins also makes its own desserts on site, and every Monday and Tuesday after 4 p.m., kids 12 and under get a free kids' meal. Let your kiddos build their own hamburgers and watch them light up.

900 Dupont Road/9112 Outer Loop, (502) 897-9684
ILoveCousins.com
East End
Family Friendly

HAVE COCKTAILS AND PEOPLE WATCH
AT THE BACK DOOR

On a business trip years ago, I told an attractive sales rep who was wooing me with dinner and drinks that if she ever came to Louisville, I would take her to the Back Door. Let's just say the deal fell through, but the Back Door, located in a rear corner of the Mid-City Mall in the Highlands, is a dive everyone should visit at least once. (Hey, it was on *The Tonight Show* one time; show some respect.) Get there early so you can get a seat, order some of the most reasonably priced drinks in town, and just take in the show. You'll see a parade of hipsters, bikers, weirdos, middle-aged couples on their way to a movie, geeks, coeds, and punks as they come and go until 4 a.m. or until you pass out, whichever comes first. You might score a drunken makeout. Oh, and plan to take a cab home because the Back Door doesn't mess around when making a gin and tonic.

1250 Bardstown Road, (502) 451-0659
TheBackDoorLouisville.com
Highlands

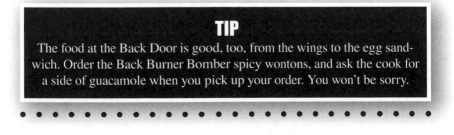

TIP
The food at the Back Door is good, too, from the wings to the egg sandwich. Order the Back Burner Bomber spicy wontons, and ask the cook for a side of guacamole when you pick up your order. You won't be sorry.

BUY SOME DRIED MEAT
FROM THE JERKY GUY

Rusty has been making homemade beef jerky for years. He then carefully places it into small Ziploc bags, wanders around the bars and eateries in Louisville's Highlands, Clifton, and Crescent Hill neighborhoods (and beyond) selling his wares to anyone craving a snack. Rusty is always wearing a straw hat, overalls, and carrying a wicker basket, so you can't miss him. He'll just stand around, say hello to the owners or bartenders, and wait for people to spot him. It's $5 a bag, and you can get everything, from sriracha to soy to habanero flavored.

Highlands/Clifton/Crescent Hill
(no one really knows)

TIP

If you like the hot stuff, look for the baggies with the running antelope and flames. The more flames, the higher the heat level.

VISIT COPPER & KINGS,
A DISTILLERY OF A DIFFERENT KIND

Yes, yes, we all know Kentucky is the home of bourbon, but in the Butchertown neighborhood sits a different kind of distillery: Copper & Kings American Brandy Distillery. Not only does this huge orange-and-black structure make delicious brandy that gets distributed far and wide, but it also plays host to community events, has a built-in fire pit and pig roast pit, and a tasting room with a view of downtown that will knock your socks off (or was that the brandy?). These cool folks even play rock music to the brandy barrels as they age in rick. We can only assume that helps the flavor profile.

1111 E Washington Street, (502) 561-0267
CopperandKings.com
Butchertown

TIP

Looking for a good, old-fashioned bourbon distillery to visit? Look no farther than Peerless Distilling (KentuckyPeerless.com), just a few short miles away in the Portland neighborhood. It's a fourth- and fifth-generation reimagining of a classic Louisville brand.

CHOW DOWN ON AN OLLIE BURGER
AT OLLIE'S TROLLEY

Ollie's Trolley is a bit of a mystery; the chain began in Miami in the 1930s, and by the 1970s it was a national treasure of sorts. There once were at least a dozen locations in the Louisville area, but now there is only one—and it is one of just a few left in the country. The tiny burger stand looks like what it says it looks like: an old-time trolley car. The side of the car even says "3rd and Kentucky Link," as if it were an actual working trolley. Inside is a window where you order and a window where you pick up your Ollie Burger with the tasty special sauce and fries with the special seasoning. If more than three or four people are in line, you'll have to wait outside the tiny structure. Whether you take it home or eat in your car, it's a reconnection to an Americana classic. (And check out Dizzy Whiz for another Louisville original.)

978 South 3rd Street, (502) 583-5214
Facebook.com/OlliesTrolley
Downtown
Family Friendly

DRINK WINE ON A BUS
AT THE F.A.T. FRIDAY TROLLEY HOP

A signature Louisville event since 2004, the F.A.T. Friday Trolley Hop event draws thousands of people the final Friday of every month to enjoy free trolley rides to area shops, restaurants, and galleries along the Frankfort, Mellwood, and Story Avenues corridor. Many of the galleries and shops will have free food samples, and wine can even be found along the way. The route continues to expand into downtown and beyond; if we're lucky, by 2020, the Trolley Hop might go all the way to Lexington.

Frankfort Avenue, FatFridayHop.org
Crescent Hill/Clifton

Image Credit: Cassie Bays

ATTEND
A BEER FESTIVAL

Yes, Louisville loves its bourbon, but boy, oh, boy, it also imbibes beer. In addition to the ever-growing number of breweries, the city also plays host to several beer festivals, such as the Tailspin Ale Festival, a February "winter warmer"; the Fest of Ale each spring; the Highlands Beer Fest and Brew at the Zoo in mid-summer; and the Louisville Brewfest every fall. You can taste-test hundreds of beers, from local to international, including some hard-to-find stuff, such as Founders Kentucky Bourbon Stout. (Do get a driver, though, as these things can get a little sloppy after the 40th or 50th sample.)

Tailspin Ale Fest, TailspinAleFest.com

Highlands Beer Festival

Brew at the Zoo, LouisvilleZoo.org

Fest of Ale, KegLiquors.com

Louisville Brewfest, KeepLouisvilleWeird.com/brewfest

Derby City Brewfest, DerbyCityBrewfest.com

MUSIC AND ENTERTAINMENT

ATTEND
A WATERFRONT WEDNESDAY CONCERT

What started as a friendly little concert on a side patch at Louisville's massive Waterfront Park has become a full-blown monthly summer event during which thousands of people meander downtown to listen to bands and be seen with all the cool kids on the third Thursday of the month, April through September. Local public radio station WFPK puts on the event, with acts ranging from Old 97's to Ra Ra Riot to They Might Be Giants. And? It's free.

Big Four Lawn, (502) 814-6500
WaterfrontWednesdays.wfpk.org
Downtown
Family Friendly

TIP
Have your picture taken with Micah, the friendly, violin-playing local who shows up to pretty much every event in town. He is a Waterfront Wednesday mainstay.

GET BLOWN AWAY
BY THUNDER OVER LOUISVILLE

Fireworks are an Independence Day tradition, but in Louisville, officially beginning in 1989, they also became a Kentucky Derby Festival kickoff tradition. Each year some 600,000 people line up along the waterfront to watch one of the largest fireworks displays on the planet fired off from the downtown Clark Memorial Bridge. During the day, aircraft of all types zoom by overhead, and food and beverage vendors serve the star-struck masses. The whole thing is really kind of insane, with enough firepower to singe eyebrows, but if you find the right vantage point—say, a private party on a rooftop or overlook—it's quite beautiful to behold.

Waterfront
Downtown
Family Friendly

GO TO THE
NATIONAL JUG BAND JUBILEE

Jug music is a distant cousin to jazz and is a truly American art form. More importantly, it was at least partially invented in Louisville. It's fitting that the city plays host to the National Jug Band Jubilee each year, drawing performers and attendees from around the country to come out and listen to this most fun and winsome of musical forms. One mainstay attraction is Louisville's own Juggernaut Jug Band, which has been keeping jug music alive since the late 1960s. Hey, it isn't often you get to see a washboard, a kazoo, and a fiddle rock out together.

Waterfront Park, (502) 417-1107
JugBandJubilee.org
Downtown
Family Friendly

TIP
Want to learn more about jug music? Local author Michael Jones has the answer. Check out his book *Louisville Jug Music: From Earl McDonald to the National Jubilee.*

SHOP LIKE A ROCK STAR
AT GUITAR EMPORIUM

Do you know where rock stars go when they're in Louisville for a concert? They go to Guitar Emporium. Why? Because, founded in 1975, Guitar Emporium is legendary for its vintage and unique guitar and amp selection. That's why the likes of U2, Bob Dylan, the Rolling Stones, ZZ Top, and more make a shopping stop when they're in town. As a teen, Guitar Emporium founder Jimmy Brown restored and sold guitars to the likes of Keith Richards, Eric Clapton, and Pete Townshend, and he parlayed it into a business that is a rock legend in its own right. Even if you don't play, you can browse the rows upon rows of guitars hanging from the walls (don't touch!) and buy some guitar picks. You know, just in case.

1610 Bardstown Road, (502) 459-4153
Guitar-Emporium.com
Highlands

ROCK OUT
AT FORECASTLE

Forecastle Festival started as a small music fest in a park and has grown to be one of the country's best known festivals. Artists ranging from Beck to Modest Mouse to Flaming Lips to Weezer to Prince have performed there. Held on an 85-acre riverfront plot, it's become quite the place to be every summer. In fact, it's not unlikely as a Louisvillian to be asked, "Do you have your Forecastle tickets yet?" Yeah, it's that prevalent. Move over Bonnaroo; Forecastle is where it's at.

Waterfront Park, ForecastleFest.com
Downtown

TIP

Get the music started one week early at Poorcastle, the all-local precursor that is designed for anyone whose budget doesn't allow for major music festivals or who just can't wait one more week for live music. If you can't afford the five bucks entry fee (which goes to support local community radio), they'll let you in free.

WORSHIP HUNTER S. THOMPSON
AT GONZOFEST

Hunter S. Thompson, the founder of the gonzo journalism movement, was a Louisville native, and every April the city celebrates his life and work with GonzoFest, a music, poetry, and art festival on the waterfront. The event features guest speakers, and in 2015 Thompson's friend Bill Murray was asked to attend, with the promise of making him a Kentucky Colonel (it didn't work). Plenty of good beer is also available because Thompson did like his beer!

Waterfront Park, (502) 744-7679, GonzoFestLou.com
Downtown

GET DOWN WITH SAUCE ON YOUR FACE
AT THE BLUES, BREWS AND BBQ FESTIVAL

People in Louisville love barbecue. The city is just Southern enough to be a solid barbecue town, with plenty of great food trucks and restaurants featuring varying styles, from Carolina to St. Louis. But every July Louisville adds Memphis and New Orleans blues to the recipe, as dozens of bands collide with hundreds of barbecue masters at the Blues, Brews and BBQ Festival. There's also a craft beer tent with tasting opportunities. So, rock to the music and eat smoked meat with your hands on the riverfront at the historic Water Tower Park, backdropped by a National Historic Landmark in the city's original pumping station and water tower built in the mid-1800s.

3005 River Road, (502) 583-0333
LouisvilleBluesandBBQFestival.com
Clifton
Family Friendly

GO BOWLING, ROCK OUT
AT LEBOWSKI FEST

The 1998 Coen Brothers film The Big Lebowski really has nothing to do with Louisville, but it is only in Louisville that you can attend the original Lebowski Fest. The two-night fest includes movie night, consisting of live music and a screening of the film, and bowling night, which also features a costume contest. Now in many cities, at Lebowski fest, you will see plenty of "Dudes," lots of beer, and sometimes stars of the film even stop in. The fan fest even has a book and film in its honor and has been written about in everything from *SPIN* magazine to *Rolling Stone*. (Note: Lebowski Fest organizers cannot get you a toe. Sorry!)

Venues Vary, (502) 583-9290, LebowskiFest.com

SEE A PLAY
AT ACTORS THEATRE

Founded in 1964, Actors Theatre of Louisville is an internationally known, award-winning theater that has staged Pulitzer Prize–winning productions and played host to resident actors, such as Kathy Bates and Kevin Bacon. It is housed in the historic original Bank of Louisville building and well known for its long-running series Humana Festival of New American Plays. The three-theater complex also features a gorgeous lobby that serves as an art gallery, and a downstairs rathskeller-style bar and restaurant. If you're around in the fall, be sure to catch the annual staging of *Dracula.*

316 West Main Street, (502) 584-1205. ActorsTheatre.org
Downtown
Family Friendly

SEE A CONCERT
AT THE PALACE THEATER

The Louisville Palace Theater is one of those places you must see to appreciate. Opened in 1928, the gorgeous theater was built in a Spanish baroque motif with 139 sculptures of the faces of historical figures, a domed ceiling with a night sky rendering, a beautiful lobby with a bar, and a 2,700-person seating capacity. From the moment you see the classic façade with its vertical, neon-lettered sign, you'll want to see a show. My life was changed forever by a John Fogerty concert there, and the list of musicians who've played the Palace over the years is beyond awesome. You have to see it once. At least.

625 South 4th Street, (502) 583-4555
LouisvillePalace.com
Downtown
Family Friendly

TIP

There's not a bad seat in the house, but you should see at least one show from the balcony to get the full effect. Feel free to hold hands with your sweetheart as you enjoy the music or a classic film during the Summer Movie Series.

MEET THE NEIGHBORS
AT GARVIN GATE BLUES FESTIVAL

Louisville is host to many big-name festivals, from the Derby Festival to Forecastle, but the Garvin Gate Blues Festival is a long-standing tradition since 1988 that is more like a neighborhood get-together (a big one). Garvin Gate is set in a small neighborhood in Old Louisville that sees its streets filled with stages, arts and crafts booths, food vendors, and lots of people every October. Legendary blues artists from all over the country come to perform, and no one is turned away. They really can't be, since the festival is literally in the streets. If you want to meet real Louisvillians (and get your groove on), this is the place to go.

500 West Oak Street, (502) 445-4193
GarvinGateBluesFestival.com
Old Louisville
Family Friendly

ENJOY TWO STATE TRADITIONS AT ONCE
AT THE KENTUCKY BLUEGRASS & BOURBON EXPERIENCE

When in Rome, right? Hey, few things are more Kentucky than bluegrass music, and this fun festival also blends in that well-known beverage made with corn and charred oak barrels. Some of the best banjo, fiddle, and guitar pickers in America come to play at the Kentucky Bluegrass & Bourbon Experience every September. Put them all together and you've got one fun weekend at Louisville's historic Water Tower Park.

3005 River Road, (502) 583-0333
KentuckyBluegrassFestival.com
Clifton
Family Friendly

SPORTS AND RECREATION

DRINK A MINT JULEP
AT THE KENTUCKY DERBY

If you come to Louisville, there is a fair chance the Kentucky Derby is in your plans. The classic horse racing event held the first Saturday of every May is self-explanatory, as is its signature cocktail, the mint julep. Don your best hat and dress or suit and bow tie, watch for celebrities on Millionaire's Row, and sip the quaint bourbon cocktail from a bonafide Derby glass. Need I say more?

700 Central Avenue, (502) 636-4400
ChurchillDowns.com
South Louisville

TIP
If you decide to sip more than a couple, do yourself a favor and have a designated driver. Derby night gets a little nuts anyway, and you don't want to add to it.

WATCH A UK VS. U OF L BASKETBALL GAME
AT A SPORTS BAR

In Louisville, college basketball is king. Once a year the hometown University of Louisville and state school University of Kentucky renew a rivalry that sets fans ablaze with trash talk, taunting, and a really good reason to drink and eat fried food. If you go to one of the local sports bars—Rootie's is a fine choice—for one of these games, get there early or you won't get a seat, and be sure to wear neutral colors if you don't have a rooting interest. Then you can watch the sea of red and blue as it ebbs and flows through the course of the game. Warning: The trash talk could get heated, but mostly it's just good, clean fun.

Recommended Sports Bars:

Rootie's
12205 Westport Road, (502) 365-4681
Rooties.com

Saints Pizza and Pub
131 Breckenridge Lane, (502) 891-8883
SaintsPizza.com

Brownie's The Shed Grille and Bar
237 Whittington Parkway (plus two other locations), (502) 326-9830
BrowniesTheShed.com

Hoops Grill & Sports Bar
6733 Strawberry Lane, (502) 375-4667

ZIP LINE
AT LOUISVILLE MEGACAVERN

For forty-two years during the middle 1900s, miners blasted limestone from beneath the city to help build roads and bridges across the Midwest. In the process, they created a massive 100-acre cavern, one of the largest in the state of Kentucky. During the Cuban Missile Crisis, it was held as a possible bomb shelter for up to fifty thousand people. Today, it is open to the public as a zip line attraction, with six zip lines, two challenge bridges, and even an underground bike course. Feel the breeze as you zip through the 58-degree cavern, or simply take a tram tour of part of the cavern's seventeen miles of passageways.

1841 Taylor Avenue, (877) 614-6342
LouisvilleMegaCavern.com
Poplar Level
Family Friendly

TIP

During the holiday season each December, the MegaCavern becomes home to Lights Under Louisville, with more than two million points of light. It's the only underground light show of its kind on the planet and was named one of the top ten Christmas light shows in the nation by *USA Today*.

SEE THE CHURCHILL DOWNS BACKSIDE,
WHERE IT ALL HAPPENS

Most people who go to Churchill Downs, Derby time or not, only see the spectacle—the beauty of the track, the horses, the paddock—but you can actually take a tour to see the barn and stable area. There you can see what really goes on during a day in the life of a thoroughbred, not to mention the trainers, jockeys, owners, and hired hands who work with these majestic creatures. Oh, and while you're there, be sure to get a cross-track photo of the Twin Spires. You can't really do that if you're sitting under them.

704 Central Avenue, (502) 637-1111
DerbyMuseum.org
South Louisville
Family Friendly

TIP

When you finish your tour, stop in at Wagner's Pharmacy right across the street and eat lunch at the counter. It's where the trainers, jockeys, and owners go. Serving the racing insiders since 1922, it doesn't get more Louisville than this place.

BIKE 20 MILES
ON THE LOUISVILLE LOOP

Louisville is a biking town. Bikers are everywhere, as are those skin-tight bike leotards that make me so uncomfortable. As such, Louisville is putting together an urban bike trail that will ultimately span about one hundred miles and encircle the city completely, and you can enjoy the topography and even some geographic history along the way. Bike one of five completed sections, or make your way from one to the other. The Loop is ever evolving, so be sure to plot your course in advance.

Louisvilleky.gov/Government/Louisville-Loop
Family Friendly

GET SOME HORSE SENSE
AT THE KENTUCKY DERBY MUSEUM

The Kentucky Derby is such a deep Louisville tradition that it has its own museum. You can make an afternoon of it by seeing the world's largest horseshoe (you can't make this stuff up), test your knowledge with Derby Trivia, be the jockey in a simulated horse race, and then have a slice of Derby pie in the museum café.

704 Central Avenue, (502) 637-1111
DerbyMuseum.org
South Louisville
Family Friendly

TIP
The Kentucky Derby Museum also has a respectable bourbon selection in the café and presents the Legends Series, a monthly tasting hosted by bourbon author Fred Minnick and featuring the top names in distilling.

WALK THE BIG FOUR BRIDGE
TO A WHOLE OTHER STATE

For years, the Big Four Bridge, a railroad truss built in 1895, sat unused near downtown Louisville, spanning the murky Ohio River for no apparent reason. But a conversion to a pedestrian bridge has turned what is now called the Big Four Walking Bridge into a tourist attraction. Including the ramps on either end, it's a little over a mile long, and it's free to walk or run across, day or night. When you find yourself in Indiana (a whole other state!), why not stroll around historic downtown Jeffersonville and check out the many shops, restaurants, and breweries? You can even get a mighty meat sandwich and a brew at a place called Big Four Burgers + Beer.

Near the 2300 block of River Road, (502) 574-3768
Downtown/Southern Indiana
Family Friendly

TIP
When you get to downtown Jeffersonville, make your way to Schimpff's Confectionary at 347 Spring Street, a store that opened in 1891. With an authentic vintage soda fountain, more candy than you can shake a cinnamon stick at, and one of the only candy museums in the U.S., your inner kid will squeal with delight.

GET "HIGH"
AT CLIMB NULU

You already know about the Triple Crown for horses, but Louisville also has a Triple Crown for human beings who like to run or walk. Running and walking events always seem to be going on in the city (weather permitting), but the Triple Crown of Running, which began in 1984, includes three distinct legs: The Anthem 5K, the Rodes City Run 10K, and the Papa John's 10-Miler, all of which happen over the course of six weeks each February and March. You might want to start training now.

1000 E. Market Street, (502) 806-8355
ClimbNulu.com
NuLu
Family friendly

SPEND A WEEKEND
EXPLORING THE PARKS SYSTEM

What some locals don't even know is that Louisville's parks system is one of the most revered in America. Designed by Frederick Law Olmstead, father of American landscape architecture and the guy who designed New York City's Central Park, the parks system by 2012 boasted 120 parks covering more than thirteen thousand acres. From golf courses to trails to aquatic parks to the nation's largest municipal urban forest (the gorgeous Jefferson Memorial Forest) to dog parks to the revitalized waterfront, there's quite literally something for everyone to enjoy. Pack a lunch.

(502) 456-8100, OlmstedParks.org
West Louisville
Family Friendly

TIP
Catch the breathtaking view of the city from the overlook at the top of Iroquois Park.

PLAY HOOKY FOR THE PRE-DERBY PARTY:
KENTUCKY OAKS

For years, the Kentucky Oaks, sort of the fillies version of the Derby, was an afterthought during the annual Derby Festival. These days the full-day racing schedule on the eve of Derby is almost as popular—at least locally—as the Derby itself. Half the city plays hooky from work, and some businesses even close down early or altogether to celebrate. If you go, dress in pink and get yourself a Lily, the easy-sipping pink vodka cranberry cocktail, in an official commemorative Oaks glass.

700 Central Avenue, (502) 636-4400
ChurchillDowns.com
South Louisville

GET A PERSONALIZED SIGNATURE BAT
AT SLUGGER MUSEUM

When J. F. Hillerich opened his woodworking shop in Louisville in 1855, he wanted to make porch columns and butter churns, but a chance request to make a baseball bat for a local professional player led to the invention of the Louisville Slugger. Today the Slugger Museum on Main Street is best recognized by the world's largest baseball bat, a six-story-tall monstrosity in front of the entrance. Inside, visitors can tour the factory and see how the bats are made, check out the classic baseball relics on display, have photos taken with a life-sized statue of Babe Ruth, peruse the wall of fame for their favorite players, and hit a few balls in the batting cages. You can even hold Babe Ruth's actual bat among others used by Hall of Famers. While you're there, have your own personalized signature Louisville Slugger made, just like the big-leaguers. Swing away.

800 West Main Street, (877) 775-8443
SluggerMuseum.com
Downtown
Family Friendly

TIP
While checking out the giant bat, take a look a half block west and see if you can spot Kentucky Mirror and Plate Glass. You'll recognize it by the giant shattered window and baseball which was made to look like it was hit through the giant window by the giant bat. Louisville does have a sense of humor.

"LOCK THROUGH"
THE McALPINE LOCKS AND DAM

Climb into your canoe or kayak, paddle up, and get moving down the Ohio River where you will soon encounter the Falls of the Ohio and an engineering marvel known as the McAlpine Locks & Dam. Originally built in 1830, its purpose is to allow barges and other craft passage to the lower portion of the Ohio River. Originally, travelers had to portage past the falls, making river commerce difficult at best. These days, barges pass almost effortlessly through on their way up and downstream. Recreational craft also can "lock through," and the experience is breathtaking, as thousands of gallons of water drain out of a lock the size of three football fields beneath you. You have to do it once.

805 N. 27th Street
lrl.usace.army.mil/Missions/Civil-Works/Navigation/Locks-and-Dams/
McAlpine-Locks-and-Dam/
Ohio River
Family friendly

TIP
The annual Mayor's Hike, Bike & Paddle happens every labor day, and hundreds of small watercraft lock through at the same time. It's a sight to behold.

GET LOST
IN CHEROKEE PARK

Nothing screams "Louisville" quite like Cherokee Park. Part of the city's incredible parks system, 409-acre Cherokee Park in the Highlands boasts such attractions as Dog Hill, where dogs romp and play; Big Rock, a picnic area by a huge rock in Beargrass Creek; Hogan's Fountain, a former dog- and horse-watering fountain located atop a hill on the Scenic Loop; the Nettleroth Bird Sanctuary; and the Scenic Loop, great for biking, hiking, or driving through the park. You can even enjoy a free archery range. Wonder if Louisville native Jennifer Lawrence ever practiced there to prep for *The Hunger Games?*

745 Cochran Hill Road, (502) 456-8100
OlmstedParks.org
Highlands
Family Friendly

EXPERIENCE
THE TRINITY VS. ST. X FOOTBALL RIVALRY

Over the years, Trinity High School's football teams have been state champions twenty-three times. St. Xavier, Trinity's cross-town rival, boasts the most successful athletic program in the state with more than 175 total state titles across all sports, and when they meet under the Friday night lights each autumn, it is absolute civil war. The annual showdown that began with Trinity's inception in 1956 is one of the most highly attended regular season football games in the U.S., drawing more than thirty thousand fans at Papa John's Cardinal Stadium each season. Pep rallies, bonfires, and tailgating are the order of the day, and the electrified atmosphere is that of a Division I college bowl battle. Get ready for kickoff. (Cue referee's whistle . . .)

2800 S. Floyd Street
South Louisville
Family Friendly

SPACE OUT
AT THE RAUCH PLANETARIUM

Like to chill out under the stars? At the Gheens Science Center and Rauch Planetarium, you can do it indoors. The planetarium is an educational tool at times, an entertainment venue at others. When it's not educating students from the University of Lousville or there for a field trip, or offering visual presentations about things like black holes, you can see a laser show paired with artists like the Beatles, Pink Floyd, and others.

106 W. Brandeis Avenue, (502) 852-6664
Louisville.edu/planetarium
University of Louisville
Family Friendly

EAT A DOUBLE STACK FRIED BOLOGNA SANDWICH
AT SLUGGER FIELD

You've seen baseball before; it's the game where nine guys stand around until someone launches a ball into a cleanly shorn meadow. Louisville Bats baseball, however, is played at one of the sweetest minor league ballparks in America, a wonderland where the grass is emerald green, the beer is cold and affordable, and you can get a fried bologna sandwich. Even better? You can get a *double stack fried bologna sandwich.* That's right: two wholesome, nutritious hunks of processed meat parts on Wonder Bread, topped with mustard and onions and whatever else you want. Warning: You *think* you can make the same sandwich at home, but you can't. It's a ballpark thing. Don't even try to understand it.

401 East Main Street, (502) 212-2287
BatsBaseball.com
Downtown
Family Friendly

TIP

Louisville is a big soccer town,
so if you patronize the Bats, you'd be remiss
if you don't attend a Louisville City FC
(LouisvilleCityFC.com) soccer match.
Try to get a seat in the home boosters section.
It's *electric!*

TAILGATE
AT A UNIVERSITY OF LOUISVILLE
FOOTBALL GAME

A rite of fall, tailgating is almost as important as the game itself when the University of Louisville Cardinals play at Papa John's Cardinal Stadium. In fact, the pregame activities may even be more important. Some people show up to tailgate even when they don't have a game ticket so that they can imbibe with friends, pitch a tent in the massive parking lot, and grill brats and burgers. One thing is for sure: if you go, you are definitely going to see someone you know. Even if you go alone.

2800 South Floyd Street, (502) 852-2779
PJCardinalStadium.com
South Louisville
Family Friendly

TIP
There's no tailgating in basketball, but catching a sporting event at the downtown Yum! Center provides a good time as well. Go early so that you can grab a drink or a meal at one of the many nearby bars and restaurants.

CHECK OUT
THE WORLD'S LARGEST LIVESTOCK EXPO AND RODEO

If Noah were still alive, he'd probably go to the North American International Livestock Exposition. Each November visitors from more than a dozen countries visit the event known as "the world's largest, all-breed, purebred livestock expo," held in Louisville since 1974. This is where the world's largest beef and sheep events occur, not to mention everything from boer goats to llamas. Part of the fun is the North American Championship Rodeo and the Giant Country Store, featuring hundreds of vendors peddling all sorts of wares, from handcrafted furniture to boots. Yee-haw.

Kentucky Fair and Exposition Center, (502) 367-5293
LiveStockExpo.org
Highland Park
Family Friendly

CULTURE AND HISTORY

HAVE YOUR PICTURE TAKEN WITH COL. SANDERS
AT THE DOWNTOWN VISITORS CENTER

You might want to get your Louisville visit started at the Visitors Center at 4th and Jefferson, where you can buy tickets to local attractions, find out where the best restaurants are, and even get an itinerary created just for you. Get things started by having your picture made with the iconic Col. Harlan Sanders statue, which is so popular that his suit is continually being dry-cleaned. Don't worry, though, because according to the convention and visitors bureau's Stacey Yates, the Kentucky Fried Chicken founder's likeness is never left in the buff. He has two suits to spare him (and you) the indignity. Note: The chicken in the bucket the colonel is holding isn't real, so don't try to eat any.

301 South Fourth Street, (502) 379-6109
GoToLouisville.com
Downtown
Family Friendly

TIP
While you're there, walk due south and check out 4th Street Live. Yeah, it's touristy and mostly filled with chain restaurants and bars, but at least you can tell your friends you saw it.

GET KNOCKED OUT
AT THE MUHAMMAD ALI CENTER

The award-winning Muhammad Ali Center downtown is more than just a museum; it is an educational journey of sorts that carries with it a message about how to be the best one can be. Those approaching downtown on Interstate 64 get the ultimate first impression. From the west, a mosaic on the side of the building depicts the legendary boxer's face. From the east, a mosaic shows Ali boxing. Watch one of his greatest fights or shadowbox with him in the Train With Ali exhibit. Trust me, you'll be knocked out.

144 North Sixth Street, (502) 584-9254
AliCenter.org
Downtown
Family Friendly

SPEND A DAY
AT THE LOUISVILLE ZOO

The Louisville Zoo is a must-see family attraction that goes back to 1969, and it's more than meets the eye. The zoo currently exhibits more than 1,500 animals on 134 acres, with such attractions as a gorgeous vintage carousel and an annual Halloween party. One of the zoo's more overlooked features is a small Revolutionary War–era cemetery with a stone border, gate, small garden, and a marker listing the names of those buried there. Attend the annual Brew at the Zoo beer festival, or visit the lorikeet sanctuary and feed nectar to the birds perching on your shoulder. Whatever the case, be sure to check in on the sea lions and polar bears. They're always a sight to see.

1100 Trevilian Way, (502) 459-2181
LouisvilleZoo.org
Poplar Level
Family Friendly

GET CULTURED
AT THE SPEED ART MUSEUM

At the Speed Art Museum, you'll find hundreds of exhibits spanning more than 6,000 years of art and culture representing all walks of the human race. The museum itself is sort of a piece of history, at least locally, as it was built in 1927 and funded by Hattie Bishop Speed to make the museum a tribute to her late husband, James B. Speed. The endowment helped set the Speed's tradition of not charging admission, a tradition that carries on with free admission every Sunday. The museum's walls are packed with American and European paintings, sculptures, contemporary art, and modernism.

2035 S. 3rd Street, (502) 634-2700
Speedmuseum.org
University of Louisville
Family-friendly

TIP
If you want a grown-ups' night out, catch After Hours at the Speed on Friday for live music and drinks.

VISIT THE HISTORIC
CRESCENT HILL FILTRATION PLANT

Back in the 1800s, most drinking water was kind of gross. Today, we would never drink the muddy stuff our forebears had to ingest. In Louisville, however, the local water company became a pioneer in researching methods of drinking water filtration, which led to the construction of the Crescent Hill Filtration plant in the 1870s. This effort was led in part by George Warren Fuller, the man known as "the father of sanitary engineering." Complete with a pair of elevated 110-million-gallon reservoirs, a gorgeous Victorian-style gatehouse, and a walking path around the perimeter, the plant became an immediate tourist attraction, with people coming from around the region by train, horse, and buggy. Today, it's a beautiful place to walk the "Mayor's Mile," gaze across the water, or have a family picnic.

Hillcrest and Frankfort avenues, (502) 583-6610
LouisvilleWater.com
Crescent Hill
Family Friendly

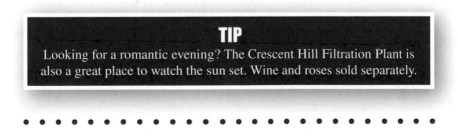

TIP
Looking for a romantic evening? The Crescent Hill Filtration Plant is also a great place to watch the sun set. Wine and roses sold separately.

GET FOSSILIZED
AT FALLS OF THE OHIO STATE PARK

When we were children, my best friend and I used to wander along the Ohio River in Clarksville, Indiana, just across from Louisville, even walking across the river bed when the McAlpine Dam was closed. We regarded the thousands of fossilized fish and other past life casually because, well, we were just kids. Today, the Falls of the Ohio State Park preserves the 390-million-year-old fossil beds that are among the largest, naturally exposed, Devonian fossil beds in the world. Visitors can wander along the shore, picnic, or take an educational tour. A really nice interactive Interpretive Center educates visitors on the preserve's history.

201 West Riverside Drive, Clarksville, Indiana, (812) 280-9970,
FallsoftheOhio.org
Clarksville
Family Friendly

TAKE A
HAUNTED WAVERLY HILLS
SANITORIUM TOUR

The Waverly Hills Sanitorium, touted as "one of the most haunted places on earth," has been featured on such shows as *Ghost Hunters* and investigated by paranormal experts the world over. For years, it's been a place for teenagers to sneak into and for paying visitors to tour or even spend the night. Around Halloween time, this former hospital, which opened in 1910 for those in the throes of tuberculosis, becomes a major attraction. Come on down, see the "death chute," hang out with the shadow people, and play ball with the little boy ghost who walks the hallways. Relax. The restless spirits here are totally friendly. Pretty sure.

4400 Pareles Lane, (502) 933-2142
TheRealWaverlyHills.com
South Louisville

TIP
Don't spend the night unless you're insane.

TOUR THE HISTORIC
STITZEL-WELLER DISTILLERY

Originally opened on Derby Day in 1935, the historic Stitzel-Weller Distillery had been closed to the public for years until 2014. Today, the Bulleit Frontier Whiskey Experience gives visitors on the Kentucky Bourbon Trail a chance to see where Julian P. "Pappy" Van Winkle Sr. created his now highly sought-after brands. In addition to the historic rick houses that still hold some four hundred thousand barrels, the Old Fitzgerald Smokestack, a tasting room, and beautiful grounds, an operating still can also be seen. Every bourbon lover will feel a genuine sense of history when inside this true cathedral of distilling.

3864, 3896 Fitzgerald Road, (502) 475-3325
BulleitExperience.com
Shively

TIP

Shively is about five miles from downtown, and many of the streets around the distillery are named after legendary Louisville distilleries. See how many names you can find, such as Farnsley and Wathen and Bernheim, before you head back to town. When you find Fitzgerald Road, you're onto something.

61

DRINK GREEN BEER
AT THE ST. PATRICK'S DAY PARADE

Louisville has a rich Irish heritage, thanks to immigrants who came here in the 1800s to build a new life. This is how Louisville's chapter of the Ancient Order of Hibernians came to be, and it's also why Louisvillians flood the Highlands each March on the Saturday before St. Patty's Day for a giant parade and the consumption of untold gallons of green beer. If you want the full experience, attend the blessing of the cask at Goodwood Brewing downtown, follow the cask to the tapping at O'Shea's Irish Pub, and then prepare for some of the best barrel-aged stout you'll ever wrap your lips around.

Baxter Avenue, LouisvilleIrish.com
Highlands

> **TIP**
> If you can't make it in March, then make plans to attend the annual Louisville Irish Fest (LouisvilleIrishFest.com) held every September at Bellarmine University. Shop Celtic crafts, drink Guinness stout, have some fish and chips, and listen to authentic Celtic music. Oh, and pray the Irish Wolfhounds are in attendance.

MARVEL AT THE HALLOWEEN DECORATIONS
ON HAUNTED HILLCREST

Every October, Hillcrest Avenue, a two-block straightaway between Frankfort Avenue and Brownsboro Road, becomes a living nightmare. OK, maybe that's a bit strong. What happens is that residents decorate their yards for Halloween and go so far that the street has become a regional holiday destination. Some of the displays look like graveyards, some feature life-size figures of movie monsters, some celebrate Area 51 aliens, and one even features undead thoroughbred race horses. It's a great place to take the kids trick or treating, but be prepared to park and walk a few blocks to get there.

Hillcrest Avenue, HalloweenOnHillcrest.com
Crescent Hill
Family Friendly

EXPLORE LOUISVILLE'S DISTILLING PAST
AT THE EVAN WILLIAMS
BOURBON EXPERIENCE

The Evan Williams Bourbon Experience may be the crème de la crème of bourbon attractions in Louisville. The first feature you see is the five-story-tall bottle of bourbon pouring into a fountain (that's hard to miss). Next, you step into a virtual, interactive historical tour starting with a walk down Louisville's waterfront as it appeared in the late eighteenth century, followed by a walk down Main Street during the city's distilling heyday on Whiskey Row, through Prohibition, and into the present, followed by a guided bourbon tasting and a stop at the Evan Williams gift store. Be sure to visit the speakeasy in the basement before you leave.

528 West Main Street, (502) 584-2114
EvanWilliams.com/BourbonExperience
Downtown

TIP
Just down the street are two more distilleries you can tour in Kentucky Peerless Distilling Co. and Angel's Envy Distillery.

STEP INTO HISTORY
AT THE SEELBACH BAR

Have a signature cocktail at the Seelbach Bar, one of the jewels of the four-star hotel built in 1869 by Bavarian brothers Otto and Louis Seelbach. This is the hotel wherein, during Prohibition, some of the country's most notorious gangsters would gather; Al Capone had a favorite alcove in one room of the hotel. He also had a huge mirror brought down from Chicago and placed strategically so that he could watch his back, and hidden doors in the room led to secret passageways for an easy escape. In addition, it was at the Seelbach that F. Scott Fitzgerald met "King of the Bootleggers," George Remus, who became the inspiration for *The Great Gatsby*. While at the hotel, take a look around the ornate lobby, and keep an eye out for the famous "Blue Lady," the hotel's legendary ghost.

500 South 4th Street, (502) 585-3200
SeelbachHilton.com
Downtown

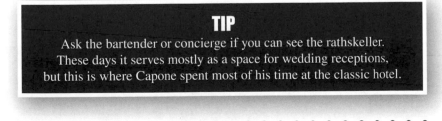

TIP
Ask the bartender or concierge if you can see the rathskeller. These days it serves mostly as a space for wedding receptions, but this is where Capone spent most of his time at the classic hotel.

VISIT MUHAMMAD ALI'S
BOYHOOD HOME

For decades, the tiny ranch-style home at 3302 Grand Ave. deteriorated. As recently as 2014, it was in danger of falling down altogether, but a real estate investor purchased the house and undertook a complete overhaul that cost about $250,000, restoring it to the way it looked in the 1950s when the legendary Louisville Lip was a teenager, complete with a bright pink coat of paint. Today, visitors can find the house easily thanks to a historical marker out front that states where Ali (then Cassius Clay) was born and chronicles his ascent to becoming "The Greatest."

3302 Grand Ave.
West Louisville
Family Friendly

HAVE A DONUT CHEESEBURGER AND PET A PIG

AT THE KENTUCKY STATE FAIR

Ah, the Kentucky State Fair. I had my first corn dog there. Three bites in, I realized it was green in the middle, but I always loved going to the farm animal competition and petting the pigs (though they really stink). It's also the home of the World Championship Horse Show, the world's most prestigious saddlebred horse competition which brings competitors from around the globe. These days one can also find bizarre food items, such as fried Twinkies and donut cheeseburgers. If you want to spend a day walking the midway and then hitting up a beer tent at night for some live cover tunes, though, there's nothing finer, and the people-watching is free. Just watch out for the corn dogs.

Kentucky Fair & Exposition Center, (502) 367-5180
KyStateFair.org
Highland Park
Family Friendly

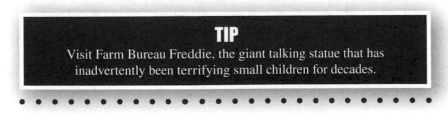

TIP
Visit Farm Bureau Freddie, the giant talking statue that has inadvertently been terrifying small children for decades.

TOUR A HISTORIC FARMHOUSE
FROM THE 1800s

Farmington, built in the early 1800s, is a great call for a Saturday afternoon family outing. You can wander the grounds of what originally was a 550-acre (it's now 18 acres) hemp plantation and tour the gorgeous farmhouse, a 14-room Federal-style home that has been restored to what it would have been like in its heyday. The home is believed to have been built based on a design created by Thomas Jefferson and Abraham Lincoln is believed to have visited there for roughly three weeks prior to becoming president.

3033 Bardstown Road, (502) 452-9920
Farmingtonhistoricalplantation.org
Hawthorne
Family Friendly

TIP
Planning a family reunion, wedding, or professional gathering? You can rent Farmington to make the event picturesque.

SEE AMERICA'S LARGEST COLLECTION
OF SHOTGUN HOUSES

Strange but true—Louisville is well known for its cathedrals, Victorian neighborhoods, and iron façades downtown, but it is also home to the largest number of shotgun houses in America. Brought about primarily in the late 1800s and early 1900s, these houses are so named because you can theoretically fire a shotgun in the front door through the house and out the back door. They were built primarily to help accommodate the hordes of incoming German and Irish settlers and are found in several Louisville neighborhoods, including Butchertown, Germantown, Clifton, Smoketown, and Portland. Preservation Louisville even has a "Save Our Shotguns" campaign to ensure the historical homes are not wantonly destroyed.

(502) 540-5146, PreservationLouisville.com
Butchertown, Germantown, Clifton, Portland
Family Friendly

GET STONED
AT LOUISVILLE STONEWARE

One of the oldest stoneware manufacturers in America, Louisville Stoneware has been a staple of the city since 1815. Take a tour and follow the steps of more than twenty skilled artisans who take the clay from raw form to completed piece. You can even paint your own.

731 Brent Street, (502) 582-1900, LouisvilleStoneware.com
Downtown
Family Friendly

TIP
Can't get your fill? Then check out other stoneware manufacturers in or near the city, such as Hadley (HadleyPottery.com) or Bybee (BybeePottery.com).

HAVE YOUR PICTURE TAKEN
IN FRONT OF THE HEIGOLD FAÇADE

In the early 1800s, one of the more affluent areas in Louisville was known as The Point. It was so close to the Ohio River, however—just a couple of miles east of downtown—that it was well within the flood plain. Enter the Great Flood of 1937, which submerged The Point and pretty much destroyed it completely. Only a couple of structures survived, one of them being the façade of the Heigold House, a mansion built by German immigrants in the 1850s. The façade was moved to its current place at the corner of Frankfort Avenue and River Road in 2007 and is now a popular spot for visitors and photo seekers.

Frankfort Avenue and River Road
Clifton
Family Friendly

TIP
Look for the marble bust at the top of the façade—that's former U.S. President James Buchanan, one of America's *least* beloved presidents. Nevertheless, the inscription reads "Hail to Buchanan, now and forever."

TAKE A HISTORIC
DOWNTOWN HOMES TOUR

Did you know that Louisville has one of the largest habitable Victorian neighborhoods in America? The Old Louisville neighborhood, built primarily between 1880 and 1905, also has the largest number of pedestrian-only streets of any other similar neighborhood in the U.S. of A. Seriously, Old Louisville is a paradise for architectural design, and one only has to park and walk around to see it. This area was also part of the Southern Exposition, held from 1883 to 1887, where Thomas Edison helped create the then-largest-ever display of incandescent light bulbs. He had previously been a Louisville resident. Stop by the Old Louisville Information Center, or schedule a guided walking tour, and be sure to check out the Conrad-Caldwell House Museum while you're at it.

1340 South 4th Street, (502) 718-2764
LouisvilleHistoricTours.com
Old Louisville
Family Friendly

TIP

Just a few miles away in Butchertown
is the Thomas Edison House,
the place where Edison lived while in
Louisville when he worked for Western Union.
The small shotgun-style house is located
at 729 East Washington Street and is
open for tours as a mini-museum.

VISIT
LOUISVILLE'S CATHEDRALS

Louisville's Catholic heritage is beautifully represented by the Cathedral of the Assumption, established in 1789 and designed with stone arches that are topped by a ceiling adorned with 24-carat gold stars. The settlers of the middle 1800s brought even more cathedrals, and over the decades the city has become home to churches of many different faiths, including Buddhism, Christianity, Hinduism, Judaism, and more. Minutes from the Cathedral of the Assumption is the Christ Church Episcopal Cathedral, a Romanesque Revival church built in 1824, and St. Martin of Tours, where visitors can view the bodies of long-dead saints. Many more religious buildings can be seen too; call it "the other spirits tour" if you're a bourbon lover.

Cathedral of the Assumption
433 South 5th Street, (502) 582-2971

Christ Church Episcopal Cathedral
421 South 2nd Street, (502) 587-1354

St. Martin of Tours
639 South Shelby, (502) 582-2827
StMartinofToursChurch.org

Downtown
Family Friendly

EXPLORE
LOUISVILLE'S ARTS SCENE

For a city much smaller than New York and even nearby Indianapolis, Louisville has a surprisingly robust and lively arts scene. It is one of only eleven cities in the U.S. where all five major cultural institutions are represented: the Kentucky Opera, Actors Theatre, Louisville Ballet, Louisville Orchestra, and the Speed Art Museum. Visual arts also has a strong presence, and the city's Fund for the Arts, founded in 1949, keeps the scene growing with its educational programs, including 400,000 art experiences provided to area children. Something is going on literally every day.

623 West Main Street, (502) 582-0100
FundfortheArts.com
Downtown
Family Friendly

GET SMART
AT IDEAFESTIVAL

Every autumn smart and creative people, including authors, scientists, and artists, get together to share their ideas with other people interested in hearing them. From the plausibility of an actual zombie apocalypse (it could happen, OK?) to a discussion of what and where the universe actually is to the rise of artificial intelligence, IdeaFestival is really just a place for people to broaden their minds in the areas of the arts, business, technology, design, science, philosophy, and education. Couldn't we all use a few good ideas?

Kentucky Center, (888) LOUISVILLE
IdeaFestival.com
Downtown
Family Friendly

SPEND A REFLECTIVE AFTERNOON
AT HISTORIC CAVE HILL CEMETERY

Opened in 1848, Cave Hill Cemetery occupies 296 acres of land that once was a farm and later a "pest house," where the terminally ill with highly contagious diseases would live their final days. This led to a cemetery on the beautiful grounds that included a spring erupting from a cave. As the Victorian era evolved, Cave Hill became a garden cemetery complete with roads and ponds. Visitors can roam the grounds, feed the ducks, marvel at the gorgeous monuments, visit the Civil War graves, and search for graves of famous people, such as Col. Harlan Sanders (some eat a bucket of chicken by his grave), George Rogers Clark, and Julian P. "Pappy" Van Winkle.

701 Baxter Avenue, (502) 451-5630
CaveHillCemetery.com
Irish Hill
Family Friendly

TIP
If you're in Louisville for bourbon culture, try to catch a historic bourbon tour of the cemetery with bourbon historian and author Michael Veach.

VISIT THE LITTLE LOOM HOUSE
WHERE "HAPPY BIRTHDAY" WAS WRITTEN

You know the song. You cried as a little kid when people sang it to you for the first time. Then you got embarrassed at a restaurant when your friends ratted you out to the server and the whole staff sang it in the middle of the dining room. What you probably didn't know was that "Happy Birthday" was written in Louisville by two school teachers. It was in 1893 when sisters Mildred Jane and Patty Smith Hill wrote "Good Morning to All," later changing it to the lyrics we all know and love. Today, the space and cabins are used to teach the history of weaving and textile arts.

328 Kenwood Hill Road, (502) 367-4792
LittleLoomHouse.org
South Louisville
Family Friendly

BLOW AN AFTERNOON
AT LOUISVILLE GLASSWORKS

Two separate glassworks studios in one building? That's right. You can take a tour, watch live demonstrations, or blow your own glass at Louisville Glassworks. In fact, did you know that Louisville has a rich glass manufacturing history? It's true. From 1850 to 1901, at least seven different glass manufacturing factories operated in Louisville, with six of them being bottle works. It was in Louisville that George Garvin Brown came up with the idea to put bourbon in glass bottles. Celebrate at Glassworks. Bottoms up.

Louisville Glassworks, 815 W Market Street, (502) 584-4510
LouisvilleGlassworks.com
Downtown
Family Friendly

ADMIRE THE CAST-IRON STOREFRONTS
ON MAIN STREET

Louisville is home to the second most number of cast-iron storefronts in America, behind only New York, which, clearly, is a slightly bigger city. In the early 1900s, however, thanks to some well-placed iron deposits southwest of the city, Louisville architects built gorgeous and lasting façades around the city and especially downtown. Many of these still exist today, and the city is slowly beginning to fully appreciate their historical value. You can too.

Downtown, Highlands
Family Friendly

TOUR FRAZIER HISTORY MUSEUM,
SEE ROOSEVELT'S "BIG STICK"

What began as a historic arms and military museum has grown to include rotating exhibits, ranging from Lady Diana's personal belongings to the history of the National Football League and even a Prohibition exhibit. You can also find some impressive artifacts. Remember Theodore Roosevelt's "Big Stick" policy that produced the phrase "Speak softly and carry a big stick"? Well, Roosevelt's original "stick"—an enormous gun he carried when on safari—is on display here. You can also see Geronimo's bow, Daniel Boone's Bible, General Custer's twin pistols, and Jesse James's revolver.

829 W Main Street, (502) 753-5663
FrazierMuseum.org
Downtown
Family Friendly

TAKE A RIVER CRUISE
ON THE *BELLE OF LOUISVILLE*

A National Historic Landmark, the *Belle of Louisville* is the oldest operating Mississippi River–style steamboat in the world. Today, you can take a public cruise and have a meal (fried chicken!), and when you're done, peer out over the river and sip a Kentucky bourbon, just like Mark Twain used to do. Don't forget to check out the boilers, and remember what Twain said: "Too much of anything is bad, but too much good whiskey is barely enough."

401 W River Road, (502) 574-2992
BelleofLouisville.org
Downtown
Family Friendly

TIP
It isn't normally part of the cruise, but if you ask nicely, the crew will take you to see the *Belle*'s steam calliope, which can often be heard playing "My Old Kentucky Home" by people walking along the river.

STAY AT A VICTORIAN BED AND BREAKFAST
IN OLD LOUISVILLE

About 150 years ago, the southern part of what is now downtown Louisville was an affluent area where bourbon barons lived in huge, gorgeous Victorian and Gothic Revival homes. One of the best known is Rocking Horse Manor, with its stained glass, pocket doors, and hand-carved mantels, but located within a few blocks are the Samuel Culbertson Mansion, Columbine Bed and Breakfast, and Bernheim Mansion to name just a few. Check out the Louisville Bed and Breakfast Association website to get started on finding a B&B to fit your tastes. Or park your car and just walk down South Third Street.

LouisvilleBedandBreakfast.org
Old Louisville

SHUFFLE WITH THE UNDEAD
AT THE ZOMBIE ATTACK

Every October Louisvillians don makeup and hit the strip on Bardstown Road to walk around like zombies. Stinking, rotting, filthy zombies. No one knows why they do it, they just do it. But what started as a deranged birthday party has become the largest zombie walk in the world, with about thirty thousand zombies eating brains in the streets annually. The event is free. Just be careful because while the zombies don't really stink some of them get stinking drunk by night's end.

Bardstown Road, LouisvilleZombieAttack.org

TIP
Around the same time of year, Louisville celebrates Halloween with the Fright Night Film Fest, featuring amateur filmmakers from far and wide and meet-and-greets with special guests from your favorite horror films. It'll scare your pants right off.

VISIT
JERRY'S ONE-MAN MUSEUM

On one level, it's like walking into a really weird dreamscape after drinking too much sake, but on another, the odd building at the corner of Frankfort Avenue and William Street in the Clifton neighborhood is also a dream come true. Piled with colorful antiques, signs, vintage cars, statues, and more (there's even a train car), this massive and retro-cool collection in plain view behind an iron fence is like a picker's pot of gold. There's even a Statue of Liberty with Richard M. Nixon's face on it. The owner, Jerry Lotz, doesn't typically sell his stuff, but if you can engage him in conversation, you just never know. (According to Thrillist.com, the Nixon Statue of Liberty used to be flipping the bird, but the church across the street complained, so Lotz changed it to a peace sign.)

1737 Frankfort Avenue
Clifton
Family Friendly

TIP

Don't reach through the fence to touch anything,
but if you see bearded Jerry outside,
feel free to say hello. He doesn't bite.

WIN A CAKE, EAT FRIED FOOD
AT A CHURCH PICNIC

Louisville is very Catholic. Really, *really* Catholic, and Catholic folks love church picnics. As such, summertime in Louisville is almost like one great church picnic. You don't even have to be Catholic to play. Just pick your favorite picnic on a Friday night, take the family, spin the cake wheel, and eat all the fried fish, fried chicken, and other deep-fried delicacies you can. For the best family fun, try St. Agnes in July for its famous Ride Night. There's also the wildly popular St. Joe's Picnic every August, which has been known to shut down parts of Crescent Hill (and it raises money to provide homes for children in need).

St. Agnes Church
1920 Newburg Road
(502) 451-2220
StAgnesLouisville.org

St. Joseph's Children's Home
2823 Frankfort Avenue
(502) 893-0241
StJKids.org

Highlands/Crescent Hill
Family Friendly

ASK SOMEONE
WHERE THEY WENT TO SCHOOL

In every other city I've visited, if you ask someone where they went to school, they will say something similar to "Ohio State" or "Central Florida." In Louisville, if you ask the same question, you'll hear perhaps "Male" or "Ballard" or something else. Why? In Louisville, no one cares where you went to college. It's a strange cultural quirk, but Louisville is a big city with a small-town feel, and your high school heritage matters. Think Mayberry on massive steroids and a terminal case of urban sprawl. Don't believe me? Go ahead, ask. I dare you.

Anywhere
Family Friendly

TIP

Part of this culture is that if anyone says they went to school in southern Indiana, they will immediately be treated like a social pariah. Never, ever admit you graduatcd from Clarksville High School.

SHOPPING AND FASHION

SPEND A DAY
IN NULU

NuLu, a historic part of the city where retailers and service industries once served most of the city, is now the East Market Street District's gallery and restaurant zone. You can literally spend an entire day: Have breakfast at Please & Thank You, hit Joe Ley's, visit the many art galleries, and then have lunch at Feast Barbecue. Afterward, shop at Gifthorse, Highland Glass, Red Tree, or Revolver, and then have a locally brewed beer at one of two breweries or a cocktail at Garage Bar. Then? Head to Mayan Café for dinner. Be sure to get the lima beans.

East Market Street, Nulu.org
NuLu
Family Friendly

BUY SOMETHING YOU DON'T REALLY NEED
AT ST. JAMES COURT ART SHOW

Founded in 1957, the St. James Court Art Show began as a fund-raiser to help pay for repairs to the St. James Court fountain, but what once was a neighborhood art fair is now a nationally recognized, juried art show that attracts 750 vendors from all over North America each October. Bring the family, bring the dog, and enjoy an ice cream cone as you stroll the courtyard shopping for everything from photographs to sculpture to jewelry. No, you don't really need that purple frog pendant, but it's St. James weekend. Treat yourself.

1387 S 4th Street, (502) 635-1842
StJamesCourtArtShow.com
Old Louisville
Family Friendly

TAKE
A GERMAN BAKERY TOUR

When German settlers made their way to Louisville in the 1800s, they brought with them German traditions, such as brewing beer and baking. As a result, Louisville is home to a number of German bakeries that have been around for generations. Start out at Nord's, in the Germantown/Schnitzelburg neighborhood, and have one of their famous maple donuts, a maple-iced longjohn with *a slice of bacon on top.* (Take a moment to catch your breath.) Then head to Plehn's in St. Matthews for Yum Yums and to Heitzmann's for a Butter Kuchen. You'll be fat and happy (and possibly wearing lederhosen) in no time.

Nord's Bakery
2118 S Preston Street, (502) 634-0931
NordsBakery.biz

Plehn's Bakery
3940 Shelbyville Road, (502) 896-4438
Plehns.com

Heitzman Bakery and Deli
9426 Shelbyville Road, (502) 426-7736
Heitzman-Baker.com

South Louisville/St. Matthews/East Louisville
Family Friendly

VISIT THE 21C LOBBY GALLERY
AND SEE THE BEJEWELED LIMO

21C is a hotel chain, but the lobby gallery in Louisville is a big attraction downtown. Visit the gallery, check out the Louisville- and bourbon-themed gift shop, marvel at the anatomically correct statue of David on Main Street (it's a selfie paradise), and gaze in befuddled wonder at the red penguins above the hotel entrance. While you're there, stop to run your fingers along the hood of the hotel's courtesy car, a limo covered in red marbles. If you have the time and appetite, have lunch or dinner at the exquisite Proof on Main, which is attached to the hotel.

700 West Main Street, (502) 217-6300
21CMuseumHotels.com
Downtown

TIP

If you're a guy, be sure to use the men's room trough in the 21C lobby, which is separated from the hallway by a two-way mirror so you can see patrons walk by but they can't see you. Trust me, it's a freeing experience.

VISIT HISTORIC GERMANTOWN/ SCHNITZELBURG,
SEE THE "DAINTY"

When the German settlers streamed into Louisville in the 1800s, many set up new lives in an area just southeast of downtown, a pair of adjacent neighborhoods that soon were called Germantown and Schnitzelburg, respectively. The neighborhoods have, in recent years, become desirable places for Louisvillians to live and play. With a number of popular bars and restaurants such as Four Pegs, Nachbar, and Hammerhead's; a brewery; and the legendary Check's Café (get the German potato salad!), there's a lot to love in this quaint area. While you're there, admire the classic architecture and stop in at Hauck's Handy Store, where an annual "dainty" contest is held. Ask to see the dainty and ask about the history of the game. You'll want to be a kid again.

Hauck's Handy Store, 1000 Goss Avenue, (502) 637-9282
Germantown/Schnitzelburg
Family Friendly

STOCK UP
AT THE BARDSTOWN ROAD FARMERS' MARKETS

You say you want fresh produce, flowers, and even farm-raised meat? You're in luck. Every Saturday morning in the Highlands, not one but two farmers' markets are in full swing. You can enjoy a fresh breakfast made right before your eyes (the omelets are amazing), pick out a few ears of corn, and even enjoy live music. At the Bardstown Road market, you get bluegrass tunes, while anything goes just up the road at the Douglass Loop Farmers' Market. Fresh food is abundant at both. Sometimes, local wine is available. Also, if you hit the Bardstown Road Farmers' Market in July, you might get lucky enough to find a vendor with Kentucky blueberries. Kentucky blueberries are *delicious.*

Bardstown Road Farmers' Market, 1722 Bardstown Road, (502) 395-1522
BardstownRoadFarmersMarket.com

Douglass Loop Farmers Market, 2005 Douglass Boulevard, (502) 384-8953
DouglasLoopFarmersMarket.com

Highlands
Family Friendly

TIP
If these two aren't enough, travel east to the Beargrass Christian Church (Beargrass.org) farmers' market. It gets crowded, but it's worth the trip.

GET LOST
IN JOE LEY ANTIQUES

Joe Ley Antiques is similar to what might happen if a flea market had a love child with the Addams Family's creepy home. Packed to the ceiling with antiques and oddities of all shapes and sizes, this three-story, 1890s schoolhouse offers up everything from vintage toys to architectural artifacts perfect for restoration projects. The quirky range of stock stems in part from the fact that owner Joe Ley has long been a supplier of restaurants looking for vintage adornments. Joe Ley's Antiques has even been a backdrop for music videos, movies, and commercials. Not to be missed (unless you're really afraid of clowns—lots of clowns here).

615 East Market Street, (502) 583-4014
JoeLey.com
NuLu
Family Friendly

SCARE UP A COSTUME
AT CAUFIELD'S NOVELTY

Thanks to Louisville Slugger Museum, Louisville is home to the world's largest baseball bat, but just a few blocks down the street hangs the world's largest vampire bat. The latter bat is part of Caufield's Novelty, a holiday and costume supply shop that has been a part of Louisville since the 1920s. Located at the edge of the Portland neighborhood in downtown, the business founded as a photography studio by Irish immigrant Keran S. Caufield is today one of the largest theatrical distributors in the nation, with thousands of items in stock, from masks to props to decorations. If it's the unusual you seek, you'll find it here.

1006 West Main Street, (502) 583-0636
Caufields.com
Downtown/Portland
Family Friendly

SPEND A DAY
AT LOUISVILLE SCIENCE CENTER

Some might think science is boring, but Louisville Science Center is anything but. It's three stories of hands-on fun for kids of all ages, from an IMAX theater to floor after floor of attractions in the realm of science, technology, health, and more. Unleash the young ones on Science in Play, and they'll find hours of educational entertainment. Science camps, workshops, and even overnight family adventures are ready and waiting.

727 West Main Street, (502) 561-6100
KyScienceCenter.org
Downtown
Family Friendly

BUY SOME HOMEMADE SOAP
AT FLEA OFF MARKET

Most flea markets focus on stuff. Lots of stuff, from crafts to collectibles to other people's junk. But the Flea Off Market is a bit different: held monthly, one can shop the goods of local vendors, from jewelry makers to soap makers, or just random people with stuff to sell, while also grabbing a bite to eat at one of several available food trucks. Flea Off has also become a place where the hip kids go to socialize. Why not be a hip kid?

1007 East Jefferson Street, (502) 552-0061
Facebook.com/TheFleaOffMarket
NuLu/Downtown
Family Friendly

VISIT THE CONCRETE LADY,
BUY A GARGOYLE

Located just a couple of miles north in Jeffersonville, Indiana, The Concrete Lady, which is clearly visible from Interstate 65, features more than four thousand statues and ornaments for sale year-round. In business since 1976, The Concrete Lady offers the largest variety of statuary in the U.S. All the statues are made on a 15-acre location nearby in Otisco, Indiana, so, if you ever wondered where all those concrete hippos and fairies and gargoyles come from, now you know, and now you can see it for yourself.

1001 Old Highway 31, Jeffersonville, Indiana, (812) 282-7742
TheConcreteLady.com
Southern Indiana
Family Friendly

HANG TEN
AT LOUISVILLE EXTREME PARK

Louisville is home to a robust skating culture, and I'm not talking about the Ice Capades. Louisville Extreme Park is a huge attraction for local kids and teens and their skateboards, with 40,000 square feet of concrete featuring numerous bowls and pipes designed for skaters of all skill levels. You can drop the kids off, or just hang out and read a book—or catch some concrete yourself. Cowabunga, dude.

531 Franklin Street, (502) 456-8100
LouisvilleKy.gov
Downtown
Family Friendly

SPEND A DAY
IN THE FRANKFORT AVENUE CORRIDOR

The Highlands gets all the hype, but if you want to enjoy a day of shopping, eating, and imbibing, plan to spend it (or a long afternoon) on Frankfort Avenue. Start with some pastries at Blue Dog Bakery, then make your way back down toward Clifton, stopping in the many shops along the way. Check out Louisville's original Carmichael's Books, and be sure to have a beer at Crescent Hill Craft House, which features forty taps pouring exclusively local and regional beers. Take a break on one of the park benches, and wait for the trains to go by, and then finish up in adjoining neighborhood Clifton with a meal at the Irish Rover or El Mundo.

Frankfort Avenue, FrankfortAve.com
Crescent Hill
Family Friendly

TIP
Yes, you can do pretty much the same thing in the Highlands, just with different stores and restaurants and probably not in the same day.

TAKE A MAIN STREET/ MARKET STREET

GIFT SHOP TOUR

Don't have time to hit all the museums on Main Street? No problem, because the museum gift shops are open to the public. Within four easily walkable blocks are ten museums and attractions on West Main and West Market Streets, and you can stop and shop to your heart's content. You can start at the far west end and drop by the Frazier History Museum shop, which features local history items and more, and make your way past the Louisville Slugger Museum (get yourself a mini-bat!), Kentucky Science Center (science!), Kentucky Museum of Art and Craft, Muhammad Ali Center, and more. And when you're finished? Stop off at Manny & Merle or Doc Crow's on East Main for a bite to eat.

West Main Street, MuseumRowonMain.com
Downtown
Family Friendly

TIP
If you do take one of the many museum tours, save your receipt because that will get you $1 off any other attraction on the trail.

CRASH THE
BROWNSTABLE BROWN GALA

A friend of mine claims he once got himself into the Barnstable Brown Gala, the annual Kentucky Derby kickoff party for celebrities and people who are way richer than you, thrown by socialite Patricia Barnstable-Brown. (Proceeds benefit diabetes research at the University of Kentucky, so I'm not judging.) My friend says he danced over to Tori Spelling at one point. Tori looked him up and down and walked away. But celebs from Boys II Men to Joey Fatone to Tom Brady to Miranda Lambert have been known to lurk at the $1,300-per-head Barnstable Brown bash along with more snooty guests than you can shake a stick at. I hear they have cocktail shrimp the size of small cats. Surely there's an unlocked window you can climb through.

1700 Spring Drive
East End

TIP
Do not anger Tori Spelling.

SUGGESTED
ITINERARIES

IT'S ALL ABOUT THE HORSES

Kentucky Derby, 50
Kentucky Oaks, 62
Kentucky Derby Museum, 57
Churchill Downs Backside Tour, 54
Wagner's Pharmacy, 55

FUN WITH THE KIDS

Louisville Zoo, 76
Comfy Cow, 14
Muth's Candies, 12
Caufields, 125
Ollie's Trolley, 28
Louisville Science Center, 126
Big Four Bridge, 58
Louisville Extreme Park, 129
National Jug Band Jubilee, 36

DATE NIGHT

Original Bristol, 16
Brown Hotel, 3
Vincenzo's, 13
Pat's Steakhouse, 17
Actors Theatre of Louisville, 43
F.A.T. Friday Trolley Hop, 29

GET YOUR DRINK ON

HISTORY

ACTIVITIES
BY SEASON

WINTER

Tailspin Ale Festival, February, 31

North American International Livestock Exposition, November, 71

UK vs. U of L Basketball Game, December, 51

Lights Under Louisville, December, 53

Louisville Triple Crown, February/March, 59

FALL

Kentucky Bluegrass & Bourbon Experience, September, 47

Louisville BrewFest, September, 31

University of Louisville Football, September, 70

IdeaFestival, September, 99

Trinity vs. St. X Football Game, October, 66

National Jug Band Jubilee, October, 36

Dracula at Actors Theatre, October, 43

Garvin Gate Blues Festival, October, 46

Waverly Hills Sanitorium Tour, October, 81

Louisville Irish Festival, October, 84

Zombie Attack Walk, October, 107

Haunted Hillcrest, October, 85

SPRING

St. Patrick's Day Parade, March, 84

GonzoFest, April, 40

Thunder Over Louisville, April, 35

Barnstable Brown Gala, April, 132

Fest of Ale, April, 31

Derby Festival, April–May, 62

Derby City BrewFest, May, 31

Kentucky Oaks, May, 62

Kentucky Derby, May, 50

SUMMER

Louisville Bats Baseball, April–September, 68

Church Picnic Season, June–August, 110

Summer Movie Series at the Palace, June/July, 45

Highlands Beer Festival, July, 31

Forecastle Festival, July, 38

Lebowski Fest, July, 42

Blues, Brews & BBQ Festival, July, 41

Kentucky State Fair, August, 89

Brew at the Zoo, August, 31

INDEX